They Never Gave Up

Hoyt R. Wilson

This book is a free gift to you from a donor who says,
Never give up!
Become all that you can be.

They Never Gave Up

Copyright 2010 by Hoyt R. Wilson
Second printing September, 2011

Library of Congress in Publication Data
Wilson, Hoyt R.
They Never Gave Up, illustrated by Charles Shaw
104 pages includes index and related resource information.

Summary: This book summarizes the lives of six famous Americans (Susan B. Anthony, George W. Carver, Thomas A. Edison, Abraham Lincoln, Sequoyah, and Harriet Tubman) and the hardships they overcame to become heroes we continue to admire today.

ISBN 0-9706429-0-3
1. Character development, persistence, personal values. Children's literature.
2. United States- History- Biography
Shaw, Charles, ill.   II. Title
(920-dc)   LOC Card Number: 00-193094

This book is dedicated to six fabulous girls:
Mary Brennan, Helen Catherine, Annie, Helen,
Margaret, and Caroline
plus
one remarkable boy,
Matthew

Fall seven times, stand up eight.
—Japanese proverb

They Never Gave Up

Susan B. Anthony spent her life working to gain for women the right to vote.

"We are here to register and will return to vote on Election Day."

Susan B. Anthony

A small group of frightened women huddled at the entrance of a neighborhood butcher shop in Rochester, New York. They were not there to buy meat.

A brisk fall wind picked up stray papers and danced them in the air.

A woman in the group tilted her head to the one next to her, "What will your husband say when he finds out you are part of this group?"

"I don't know but he won't be pleased."

Other women in the group looked at each other and nodded. They understood. But here they were, both excited and scared as they waited for their leader, Susan Anthony.

It wasn't long before Susan walked up, smiled at the women, and greeted each of them by name. She asked, "Are you ready to make history?"

Their fears fell away as they followed her into the shop where men in that section of town signed up to vote.

Walking quickly to the man seated behind a small table in the corner of the shop, Susan spoke in a firm voice, "We are here to register for the election."

The man could not believe what he heard. He looked up from the voting ledger with a shocked expression on his face. He said in a strained voice, "You what . . . you want to vote? That's impossible. Women can't vote!"

Susan looked straight into his eyes and said, "The Constitution says all United States citizens can vote. We are here to register and will return to vote on Election Day. Please register us now."

This scene that took place in 1872 seems strange to us today. But life for women in America was much different then than it is today. The Civil War had ended seven years earlier in 1865. Soon after that, Congress passed the Thirteenth Amendment to the Constitution, which abolished slavery, and the Fourteenth Amendment, which granted voting rights to all citizens both white and black.

But life for women did not change. They were not allowed to vote. Most colleges were closed to them. If married and working outside the home, they could not collect their wages, which were paid instead to their husbands.

The few jobs available to women included sewing, teaching, house cleaning, or working in a textile factory. It was unfair and frustrating, and Susan Brownell Anthony was about to change all of that!

Susan Anthony was born in Adams, Massachusetts, on February 15, 1820. Her parents believed that men and women should have the same rights. What men could do, women should have the right to do also. That belief influenced Susan throughout her life.

Her patents instilled in her the desire of learning. Susan was very bright and learned to read and write by the age of three. When she was six years old, the family moved to Battensville, New York, where her father started a school in their home for his children and those of the neighbors.

As she got older, Susan prepared to be a school teacher. Her father said, "Susan, you are smart with a good speaking voice; ideal qualities for a teacher."

"But father, I'm not sure that's what I want to do. There is something else for me."

"Marriage?"

"No father. It's fine for other women to be homemakers, but I have no interest in keeping house for a husband and children."

"What then?"

"Well, I want to do things that help women gain the same rights that men have."

Her time and effort became focused on women's rights from that point on.

At the age of 32, Susan made the trip to the meeting of the Sons of Temperance in Albany, New York. This group opposed the sale and drinking of alcoholic beverages. She listened to the discussion and waved her hand to be recognized. She certainly was not timid.

A man in back of her grabbed a hand full of her dress and attempted to jerk her back into her seat. She pulled loose and remained standing. The man at the podium said in a gruff voice, "Madam, please be seated. The women were invited here to listen and learn, not to speak."

Susan was stunned!

The man continued, "Women should share their thoughts with a man who will then do the speaking."

That didn't sit well with Susan. She thought *I have things to say, and I intend to say them!!* You could feel tension in the air.

Men shouted, "Take care of your husband and children. A woman's place is in the home!"

She didn't like what she heard. But she was shut off from further comment. She moved on to other gatherings including a teachers' convention where she demanded for women the same rights and privileges enjoyed by men. Again she was ignored.

Men asked, "Who is this woman trying to cause us trouble?"

After similar reactions at several meetings, Susan spent time thinking about the way she was treated. She realized something. In her mind she saw the answer. Women must have the right to vote! They couldn't make changes unless they could vote for those changes. That became her obsession; her direction in life.

"Women's place is in the home."

Susan's days and nights were soon filled giving speeches to groups of women; large or small, it didn't matter. She crossed America and spoke to all who would welcome her. Her work was difficult, but she never wavered from this new direction in her life.

She became a close friend with Elizabeth Stanton who also was working for the rights of women. Elizabeth was married with children, but she set aside time to work with Susan.

They became a team and enlisted 10,000 women to sign a paper that requested a law giving women in New York the right to own property.

"Here, sign this petition. If we can get enough signatures, the legislature will have to consider our request."

Strange as it seems to us today, women at that time could not own property.

They took the request to the legislature in Albany. One man said, "What's this petition?"

"Oh, a group of women here are asking us to change the law and allow them to own property."

The first man laughed and said, "Well that's not going to change."

The lawmakers listened half-heartedly and refused to act. Women sitting in the balcony were very still and listened to the exchange on the floor of the assembly. They were discouraged. Susan was not! With a strong voice she told the legislators, "We are not quitting! We will keep coming back until laws are passed that give women the rights that they deserve."

Over the next several years Susan secured signatures on more petitions and returned to Albany six more times. Finally on the seventh trip, she and her supporters were successful! The New York legislature passed a law in March, 1860, granting women the control of the money they earned

9

and the right to own property. Susan Anthony and those who labored with her were overjoyed!

Some success at last . . . but more struggles lay ahead.

The battles and killing of the Civil War ended in 1865. The nation set about to re-establish peace and passed a constitutional amendment granting blacks the right to vote. Susan attempted to have included in the Fourteenth Amendment a statement that would give women as well as blacks the right to vote. Her efforts failed. Again she was frustrated. She thought for a long time, *now what can I do?*

She wandered along the streets of Rochester thinking, *how can this be changed?* Then like a flash, it came to her! She had an idea. A plan that would force a decision about women's right to vote. She hurried back to the house and read again the wording of the Fourteenth Amendment. There it was! She thought, *why it's been there the whole time. Now I know what to do.*

Now we go back to where this story began. On November 1, 1872, Susan led 15 women to a shop on West Street in Rochester, New York. That was the place where men in that section of town signed up to vote. She stunned the registrar when she exclaimed, "We are here to register for the election."

The man sat there in disbelief. He finally replied, "Women can't vote. It's illegal."

Susan handed him a copy of the United States Constitution and asked him to find a single line that said women can't vote. She continued, "It says all persons born or naturalized in the United States are citizens. Women are citizens!"

The registrar was put on the spot. He was angry. And, he was frightened. What could he do? He didn't want to register the women. But he did. Now that their names were added to the list of voters, the women went home. They returned on

Election Day and voted. The women were happy, but most men across America were very unhappy.

Newspapers carried the story, "New York Women Vote!!" Articles were written that read, "Those women have broken the law; they should be arrested and put in jail."

Susan waited. She remained at home and spent several days looking out her front window. The weather in Rochester was turning chilly. Trees barren of leaves waited for the cold days of winter. She awaited a chilly storm of a different type. She knew it was coming. She actually counted on being arrested and put on trial. It was in her plan; a plan to use the courts to challenge the United States' voting laws.

The waiting stretched into two weeks. Then one day a United States marshal appeared at her front door with an order for Susan's arrest.

The marshal said, "It will be less embarrassing if you appear at the courthouse on your own."

Susan stood up straight. Unafraid. Excited. She wanted to draw attention to the case so she said, "Oh no! I would rather go with you and would prefer to be taken in handcuffs."

The marshal was speechless! He didn't use handcuffs, but he did take Susan to the courthouse where her 15 voting friends were waiting. Charges were made, the women were released, and their trial was scheduled for the following summer.

The trial would be held in Rochester. Susan knew the jurors would be chosen from that county. So, she spoke daily to tell people about the issue of voting rights for women. She wanted to gain support before the trial began.

The government was just as determined to win its case. They moved the trial to another county away from where Susan had been speaking. They also decided to bring only Susan to trial. The case of the government versus Susan B. Anthony was scheduled to begin on June 17, 1873.

The government took an unusual action. Just before the trial started, the regular county court judge was replaced by The Honorable Ward Hunt, an associate justice of the Supreme Court. Newspaper reporters wrote about this very unusual action. People across America became interested in this trial. As important as it was, it lasted only two days!

On the first day Susan's attorney, Henry Selden, made an opening statement. He asked Susan to take the stand and testify in her own defense.

The prosecutor said, "She is a woman. She is not capable to speak for herself."

Henry Selden then defended Susan's right to speak. He said, "Susan Anthony did what she did to test her legal right to vote."

The prosecutor quickly shouted, "She admits breaking the law and must be punished!"

Susan was frustrated but was not allowed to reply. Judge Hunt agreed with the prosecutor and ruled that she could not take the stand.

One final surprise took place. Judge Ward Hunt opened a file and shuffled through some papers. He began to read instructions he had written *before* the trial began. People in the court room became silent. No one moved.

Judge Hunt gave Susan a stern look. He turned to face the jury, cleared his throat, and began to read aloud. He told the jury to enter only one verdict—a verdict of GUILTY!

Susan Anthony shot to her feet, red faced and angry. Henry Selden protested the charge of a directed verdict. Judge Hunt simply ignored their reactions. He pounded the gavel for silence and told the clerk to record the guilty verdict. Then he dismissed the jury. The trial was over.

People moved slowly out of the court room. Some were happy. Some were shocked. They wondered, *how could this happen?*

The next day Susan appeared in court with her attorney to hear the sentencing. The possible punishment could amount to a fine of $500 and three years in prison. Imprisonment of a woman was indeed a serious action.

Judge Hunt ordered Susan to rise and said, "Does the prisoner have anything to say before sentence is given?" He had just made a very big mistake.

Susan glared straight at the judge and replied, "Yes, your honor, I have many things to say. In your ordered verdict of guilty you have trampled underfoot every principle of our government."

Judge Hunt realized his mistake. Every word was heard and written down by newspaper reporters.   In   an   angry voice Susan said, "My natural rights, my civil rights, my political rights are all ignored. Robbed of the fundamental privileges of citizenship, I am degraded from the status of citizen to that of subject."

The judge interrupted, "The court will not listen to you."

She continued and drowned him out. "I have been denied the right to testify in my own defense. I have been denied rights never denied in a criminal case except to slaves."

"The prisoner will sit down," the judge shouted. "You have been tried according to established forms of law."

She shot back, "Yes, your honor, but by forms of law made by men, interpreted by men, administered by men, in favor of men . . . and against women!"

Judge Hunt pounded his gavel demanding silence. Susan finished with a flurry of words, "I ask not leniency at your hands, but to take the full rigors of the law."

Judge Hunt, out of control, frustrated, and embarrassed pronounced the sentence—a fine of $100 and court costs.

Again she shouted, "I will never pay a penny."

Henry Selden took Susan by the elbow and removed her quickly from the courtroom. As it turned out, Susan never did pay the fine or go to jail. Judge Hunt deliberately did not sentence her to jail. If he had done so, Susan would have appealed her case to the Supreme Court. That was part of her plan all along.

"You have been tried according to established forms of law."

The trial was two short days. It became one of America's most famous trials. It involved the voting rights of half the United States' population. She did not receive justice, and people knew it. Support for her was expressed in newspaper articles throughout the land.

Susan Anthony continued her work for the rights of women. In a short time things began to change. More colleges welcomed women as students. Four states passed laws giving women the right to vote.

The first World's Congress of Representative Women was held in Chicago in 1893. Women from around the world attended the meeting and stood in line to speak to their heroine, Susan B. Anthony. She was the one who inspired them!

Susan filled with energy and determination continued her work year after year. Then on her 86th birthday, though very ill and against her doctors orders, Susan attended her last public meeting. There she congratulated women on their progress and praised men who had helped her in the women's movement. With a voice filled with emotion she inspired the crowd and left them with this challenge: "Failure is impossible!"

Less than a month later, Susan Anthony died at her home in Rochester, New York. She had given her life working for a great cause.

Fourteen years after her death, in 1920, the Nineteenth Amendment was added to the United States Constitution. It granted all women citizens the right to vote.

"Failure is impossible."

Susan had said, "There never will be complete equality until women themselves help make the laws and elect the lawmakers."

Susan Anthony had championed that cause for most of her life. Now, even after her death, she had finally won her battle—the voting rights for women in America.

George W. Carver, born as a slave, became a world class botanist who introduced a new way of life for the poor farmers in the South.

Outlaws came to steal

George Washington Carver

In the early 1800's, a large number of people in America moved west to start a new life in what was called the "frontier territories." Many who moved west owned slaves who helped farm their land. There was disagreement about the spread of slavery into the frontier territories. This became a hot topic in America and one of the main issues that led to the Civil War in 1861.

A man named Moses Carver owned a 240-acre farm in the western section of Missouri. Moses opposed slavery, but he bought a slave named Mary to help with chores and be a friend to his wife, Susan. Living on a farm in the frontier country of Missouri was a lonely life.

This was the setting in 1864 when Mary gave birth to a son whom she named George. The father was a slave from a nearby farm. Life was going to be difficult for George, but through his struggles he became an American hero. This is his story.

It was late in the afternoon. Shadows already drifted across the front of the house. Young George, just a toddler, was in the yard with his mother and Jim, his 4-year-old brother. Moses Carver was in the house when he heard a noise that caused him to stop and listen. It didn't take long to know that the sound came from the hoofs of horses, and they were coming fast.

Moses Carver realized what was happening, and he didn't like it. An outlaw gang was coming. They had been to the farm before to steal what they could. Moses rushed outside, grabbed Jim, and carried him into the house. He yelled, "Mary, pick up George and get inside."

Moses snatched up a rifle and returned to the yard to help Mary but he was too late! Before Carver could reach them, the outlaws dashed into the yard, lifted Mary and George onto the back of horses, and rode away. The outlaws planned to sell them as slaves in the nearby state of Arkansas.

Carver was broken hearted. He returned to the house where his anger shifted to thoughts of, w*hat can I do?* Then he had an idea. *My friend Matthew will help me. He's a soldier just back from the war. I'll pay him to search for Mary and George and bring them back.*

The days that followed were long and sad as Moses Carver and his wife waited.

Susan asked, "Moses, any word from Matthew?"

"Nothing yet," Moses sadly responded.

Two weeks passed. Then one day the friend rode up to the house.

"Sorry, Moses. Found little George with a couple in Arkansas, but no sign of Mary."

Mary was never heard from again.

Moses and Susan Carver took care of the two boys and raised them as their own. Jim, strong and healthy, grew up helping with the harder jobs on the farm. George was small for his age. He helped Susan around the house by cooking, mending clothes, doing laundry, and working the vegetable garden.

Even at an early age, it was clear that George had a gift for growing things. Neighbors brought him sickly flowers and plants, which he nursed back to health.

George later in life said, "I lived in the woods and wanted to know every strange stone, flower, insect, bird, or beast."

This frontier territory didn't offer much for the few blacks in that area. The schools would not accept blacks so Moses Carver allowed George at 12 years of age to move eight miles to Neosho and attend a school for black children.

That was the first time George had been away from the Carvers and Jim. He was homesick, but he wanted very much to get an education. He stayed with a black couple in Neosho and agreed to help with their household chores in exchange for a place to live. Like most former slaves, he was known by his owner's name, Carver's George. Now he could change his name, and he chose to be named George Carver.

After a year, George learned as much as his teacher was able to teach. He then traveled to Fort Scott, Kansas, searching for a school where he could learn more.

In Fort Scott, George saw how much some whites hated blacks. One day he learned that a black man had been put in jail for being a friend to a 12-year-old white girl. At night a mob of white men stormed the jail, dragged the prisoner outside, placed a rope around his neck and hung him from a lamppost.

Watching from a short distance away, 14-year-old George Carver was terrified! He was so frightened that he left town immediately with this scene locked in his mind.

For the next several years, George continued his education, living in various places in Kansas and supporting himself by cooking, cleaning, and doing laundry. He added a middle initial "W" to his name.

Someone asked, "George, does the "W" stand for Washington?"

He replied, "Sure, why not?"

Many former slaves chose to rename themselves after famous Americans.

George W. Carver finished high school in 1885 at the age of 21. He was accepted to enter the fall semester at Highland College in Highland, Kansas. He saved his money and made the journey. When he arrived in Highland, college officials saw that he was black and did not allow him to enroll.

Carver was crushed. He was out of money and had no place else to go, so he worked around Highland for four years earning money at whatever jobs he could get.

He saved his money then made his way to Iowa where he started a laundry. A white minister in Iowa noticed how George worked hard with a positive attitude. They became friends.

The minister said, "George, you need to give college another try. Don't settle for something less." George took that encouragement and in September of 1890, he entered Simpson College in Indianola, Iowa.

Carver had developed a genuine skill as an artist and started the study of painting in college. His teacher recognized his ability but encouraged him to study something more practical.

She said, "George, you have real skill as an artist but you need a job that will give you a steady income. My father is a professor at Iowa Agricultural College in Ames, Iowa. I think you should go there and learn about farming."

George followed her advice, moved to Ames, and enrolled in college in the spring of 1891. Giving up his passion for art was difficult, but he soon realized he could better serve the needs of people by being an agriculturist.

He said, "I realize that God had a great work for me to do." This gave his life a new focus.

The early days at Ames were difficult. Many students called him ugly names and shoved him around. "What do you want with learning anyway? Just get along by doing what you're told."

George was not allowed to live in the student dormitory or eat his meals in the student dining hall. He said nothing. He didn't complain. He just worked hard at being a good student. He made new friends and was actively involved in nine college organizations ranging from the debate team to the National Guard. He received a first-rate education at Iowa State where two of his teachers later became U.S. Secretaries of Agriculture.

At the age of 30, George W. Carver received his BS degree from Iowa State. A department head said, "George, you are an excellent student. I want you to stay here at Iowa State and work as my teaching assistant. While you are doing that, you can work on your Master's Degree in Agriculture."

Carver was delighted with this arrangement and earned the Masters Degree two years later in 1896. He probably would have remained at Iowa State as a professor, but he had a deep feeling that he should somehow help improve the living conditions of poor black people. He thought a lot about his next move. It wasn't long before his direction became clear.

After class one day he was sitting alone when one of his professors walked up and handed him a letter. The letter was from Booker T. Washington, a famous black leader well known across the country. Washington was the president of Tuskegee Institute in Tuskegee, Alabama. The Tuskegee school offered the basic college courses but also focused on practical training that helped blacks get good paying jobs. Washington invited George Carver to join him and teach at Tuskegee. Carver smiled as he read the letter.

He wrote back to Washington, "It has always been the one great ideal of my life to be the greatest good to the greatest number of my people possible, and to this end I have been preparing myself for these many years."

Carver accepted the job at Tuskegee and arrived in the fall of 1896 to find a world he had never seen before. He was shocked by the sadness of black people in Macon County, Alabama. The white people had strange customs and laws that were enforced to keep blacks "in their places."

Restrictions kept blacks from voting, owning land, going to school, or using public restaurants. Ku Klux Klan gangs used violence to keep blacks pushed down in society. Blacks were often beaten and sometimes killed. Carver thought, *this is a hard place for blacks to live. But I'm needed here, and I'm going to stay.*

He took on a heavy workload at Tuskegee. He became the head of the agricultural department, taught a full schedule of classes, and managed the school's farms. He was especially good at teaching and starting programs for poor farmers in the area.

A shortage of money at the school forced Carver to find ways to farm that cost less. For example, he plowed soil enriching plants back into the earth instead of buying expensive fertilizer. He persuaded farmers to stop growing cotton that weakened the soil. Instead he suggested the farmers grow sweet potatoes and peanuts, which enriched the soil.

Carver shared with farmers the agricultural lessons learned at the experimental farm. At these monthly meetings in Tuskegee, farmers learned the latest methods of farming.

Some farmers said, "I learn a lot from you, but can't come to many of these meetings."

"Then I'll come to you," smiled Carver.

He loaded a wagon with farming materials and went to where the farmers lived. If they couldn't come to Tuskegee, he went to them. In 1906, this traveling school reached 2,000 people a month.

A farmer said, "This ain't gonna work."

Carver replied, "Of course it's going to work. You have to give it a chance."

"Folks around here say you knows farming."

"And I want to show you. Plant these seeds. Fertilize like I said. It's going to be a fine crop."

Carver drove his wagon from one farm to the next. At each one he talked, listened, and taught farmers a better way to grow crops.

Carver outfitted a wagon and traveled to talk to farmers and demonstrate farming methods.

One time Carver visited a group of farmers gathered at a black school in the town of Ramer, Alabama. While he was there, Carver experienced what he called "the most frightful experience of my life."

A white woman photographer was traveling through the South taking pictures of children in black schools. She went along with Carver on the trip to Ramer. One of the black teachers at the school met them at the Ramer train station after dark.

A crowd of whites who were gathered at the station watched Carver, the teacher, and the woman photographer as they climbed into a buggy and headed for the home of the teacher where she was to spend the night.

The crowd murmured. Tension was building all around.

The teacher felt uneasy about the plan and changed his mind. He thought it would be better for the photographer to spend the night in town instead of his home. They returned to Ramer where they were met by a hostile crowd. There were two black men riding in a buggy with a white woman.

The crowd became angrier and shouted threatening words. Shots were fired. Carver jumped from the buggy and ran. The photographer followed and went to the house where Carver was staying. That only made things worse!

Carver knew the situation was out of control.

He said, "We've got to get out of here and fast."

He immediately left the house, put the photographer in the buggy and followed back roads, and took her to the next train station where she spent the night.

He was frightened for his life. Afraid of being caught, he walked all night to stay away from the white mob. All through the night he heard sounds that told him the mob was nearby. He slipped along silently and made it safely back to Tuskegee.

Carver remained at Tuskegee for the rest of his life. During those 47 years he improved the way farmers grew crops. Among other achievements he became famous for the 300 different products he developed from the peanut. He was known as the "peanut man."

He became so well known that the House Ways and Means Committee in Washington sent him a letter asking him to visit. Reading the letter Carver exclaimed, "Well, I do declare!"

In January of 1921, he made his way to the nation's capitol. This was indeed a high honor. Gathered in the room that day were important congressmen from across the nation.

Carver, skinny as a rail, stood before them dressed in an old, wrinkled suit and in a squeaky voice told them about peanuts. The committee had scheduled ten minutes for Carver to speak, but they enjoyed him so much that he spoke for over an hour. They sensed they were in the presence of someone extraordinary.

Carver was so brilliant that many companies wanted to hire him. Thomas Edison and Henry Ford offered him employment at a huge salary to join their staffs.

Carver replied, "Thank you for the kind offer, but my work is here at Tuskegee."

He remained at Tuskegee receiving a very small salary of $1,500 a year. He remained committed to help the small Southern farmer. He referred to his laboratory as "God's little workshop," and Carver prayed each time before stepping inside.

He once told an audience, "To those who have not learned the secret of true happiness, which is a close relationship with God, begin now to study the little things in your own backyard—going from the known to the unknown—for each new truth brings one nearer to God."

"Study the little things for each new truth will bring you closer to God."

George Washington Carver overcame his birth as a slave and struggle with poverty. He became a world class botanist who spent his time working to improve the life of the poor Southern farmer. He helped his fellow man as few others have ever done.

Thomas A. Edison dealt with thousands of failures, but he is recognized today as the world's greatest inventor.

Alva asked lots of questions

Thomas A. Edison

A young boy who wanted to know how things work grew into a man who is recognized today as the world's greatest inventor.

The story begins in Milan, Ohio, where Thomas Alva Edison was born on February 1, 1847. He was the youngest of seven children. Young Edison, called Alva by his parents, was curious about everything. He was always asking questions. "Why do butterflies zigzag when they fly? What makes it thunder? How does water put out fire?"

Alva entered public school at the age of seven and quickly became an irritation to his teacher by asking so many questions. One day Alva, standing beside the classroom door, overheard his teacher tell the school principal that she thought Alva was retarded.

Alva told his mother what he had heard. She marched down to the school and right up to the teacher. With some well-chosen words she told the teacher what she thought then removed Alva from school. So Alva's formal schooling lasted only three months. Then his mother, a former schoolteacher, began to teach Alva at home. She believed that learning should be fun.

Alva was excited as he explored the world around him. He became so excited and learned so fast that his mother could hardly stay ahead of him.

When he was nine years old, his mother bought him a chemistry set. He had more than 100 bottles of various chemicals which he used in experiments. Alva thought, *somebody in my family is going to mess with my stuff, so I'll put a poison label on all my bottles. That'll keep them away!*

It worked!

At age 12 Alva took a job on the Grand Trunk Railway. He rode the train and sold newspapers, fruit, candy, and sandwiches to the passengers. Always one to stay busy, he also spent time in the baggage car where he conducted experiments with his chemistry set. That got him in big trouble.

Once while mixing chemicals, they caught on fire. The fire spread and set the baggage car on fire. The angry conductor roughed him up and threw him off the train along with all his belongings.

Alva couldn't ride the train anymore, so he started selling newspapers at stations along the railroad line. One day a heroic deed opened the way for his next adventure.

While Alva was selling newspapers and talking to customers, he noticed a freight car rolling toward the small son of the station agent who was playing along the rail tracks. Alva saw the danger and moved quickly. He dropped his papers, dashed forward, and grabbed the boy in time to save him from injury.

The boy was crying when Alva placed him in the arms of his father. The station agent was very grateful. He said, "Alva, you saved my son's life. Is there anything I can do for you?"

Alva was fascinated by the telegraph that the railroad used to send messages between stations. He thought for a moment, and then asked the station agent, "Will you teach me how to tap messages on the telegraph."

"I certainly will," the station agent replied.

Alva learned quickly. He was so good that at age 16 he began work as a telegraph operator on the Grand Trunk Railroad.

Edison was always interested in how things worked. When he found something that got his attention, he would take it apart, and then put it back together. Each time he learned something new.

When he was 21, he visited Congress and saw the way voting was done when a law was being approved. He thought the voting took too long. So he invented a machine that displayed the votes of legislators on a large board. He was excited, but a committee of the United States Congress showed little interest in the invention.

The committee chairman said, "The machine works too fast." He continued to explain, "The roll call vote takes at least 45 minutes, and the congressmen want that time to persuade others to vote for their proposed law which is up for approval."

After that experience Edison said, "I will never again invent anything that nobody wants. I will develop devices that are useful, dependable, and easy to repair."

On a cool fall day in 1869, Edison traveled to New York City. He was 22 years old with no money and no job. He visited the office of a stockbroker where shares of large companies were bought and sold. (If you owned shares of a company, you actually owned a part of that company.)

Edison persuaded an employee of the stock company to let him sleep on the floor and hang out in the office during the day. He said, "I'm looking for a job. Do you need help?

"What can you do?"

"I can fix things when they break."

"I'll tell you what I'll do. You can stay around here for a few days while you look for a job."

Edison was fascinated by the stock ticker and studied it carefully. It was actually a device similar to the telegraph and used to report the price of gold as the price changed up and down during the day. So it was very important to keep up with the selling price of gold throughout the day.

The stock ticker broke but Edison repaired it.

The stock ticker broke a few days after Edison arrived. Several employees tried to fix the machine but failed. They were frantic. The office had to get it working. Edison stepped up, made some adjustments, and got it working again. The office manager was very pleased and hired Edison at the huge salary of $300 a month.

Edison continued experimenting with the stock ticker to make it more dependable. The president of the company heard about the improvements. He was very impressed! He called Edison to his office and asked how much he wanted for his improvements.

Edison decided he might ask as much as $5,000 but knew he would accept $3,000. He stood in front of the president's desk and said, "Suppose you make me an offer."

The company president thought for a moment and answered, "How does $40,000 sound to you?"

Edison caught his breath, held the edge of the desk to steady himself, and replied, "Yes, I think that will be fair."

Now, at age 23, Edison used the money to build and sell stock tickers. He also studied other machines to find ways to make them work better. For example he improved the typewriter by substituting metal keys for wooden parts.

Seven years later, Edison moved to Menlo Park, New Jersey. That year, in 1876, he greatly improved the telephone by adding a carbon transmitter. People no longer had to shout into the phone to be heard.

Edison applied what he had learned from one invention to what he would work on next. That was certainly true when at age 30 he made his favorite invention—the world's first phonograph.

He learned how to make a disk that would react to the vibrations of sound. He gave his shop foreman a sketch to follow in making a strange cylinder gadget. The foreman was

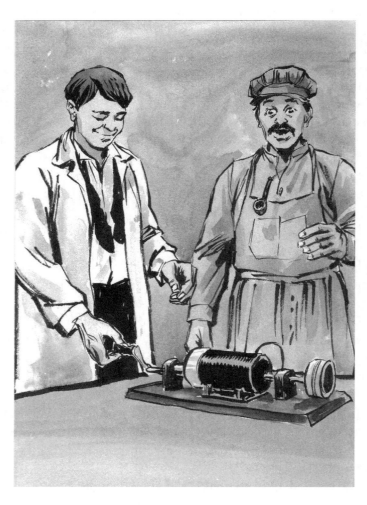

"This machine is going to talk."

puzzled and asked, "What is this crazy thing you want me to build?"

Edison smiled and replied, "Oh, this machine is going to talk."

The foreman thought, *now this I've got to see.* He constructed the gadget as Edison had directed. Edison took the strange machine and wrapped the cylinder with a sheet of tinfoil. He spoke into the mouthpiece, "Mary had a little lamb."

He started the machine which repeated his words, "Mary had a little lamb." Edison grinned but his foreman's face turned as white as a sheet.

Edison had a hearing problem that grew worse as he got older. Perhaps because of his hearing loss he spent most of his time in the laboratory away from people. But that time used experimenting produced great results.

He now faced his most difficult invention. It required patience plus hard work when he tried to invent the electric light. Edison wanted to develop a small light that could be used in the home in place of the gaslight, which was popular at the time. Edison was 32 when he began to work on the idea for the electric light. He spent two years searching for the right material to use as a filament.

The filament, or wire, had to be heated until it glowed but not burn. He sent men all over the world looking for the proper material. Hundreds of filament materials were tried. Each time they failed!

One night when everyone else was gone from the lab, Edison experimented with a mixture of lampblack and tar. When he rolled it out, it looked like a wire. He had tried everything else. He thought, w*hy not this?*

He twisted the mixture into a thin strand, put it into a glass bulb, and drew out the air. When he turned on the electric current, the bulb glowed for a brief time before burning out.

Edison thought, *I'm getting close.* He reasoned that the filament burned out because it contained air. So he took cotton sewing thread, burned it to an ash to remove the air, and then made the ash into a filament. Many more failures followed before he placed the latest filament in a bulb on October 19, 1879, where he turned on the current, and the light bulb glowed with a good light.

Edison and his helpers watched breathlessly. Minutes turned into hours. Hour by hour they waited. As daylight came the next morning, the bulb still glowed. No one wanted to sleep. They watched and waited. It continued to glow all that day and through the night. Everyone in the shop was sleepy and excited at the same time. They yawned, stretched, walked around, and waited.

The bulb continued to glow for two whole days and nights. Finally, in the afternoon of the third day, Edison increased the electricity. Only then did the bulb burn out.

The news spread quickly. The world was astounded at the invention of the electric light.

Edison became known as the Wizard of Menlo Park. This was his greatest invention!

Edison moved his laboratory from Menlo Park to a larger site in West Orange, New Jersey. This location provided more space for experiments. There he spent most of his time improving his earlier inventions and starting companies that manufactured and sold them.

In his new laboratory, Edison contributed to motion pictures by improving the camera which was invented by George Eastman. By 1914, he had combined the camera and phonograph to make talking pictures. He hoped to see this used as a teaching tool in school classrooms.

The light continued to glow.

Some of Edison's later work included the cement mixer, dictating and duplicating machines, and the storage battery. A friend once tried to encourage him when 10,000 experiments with a storage battery didn't work. Edison replied, "I have not failed. I've just found 10,000 ways that won't work." That was his attitude for success!

From his first invention, the vote-recorder, to his last, a method of making synthetic rubber, Thomas Edison contributed to society as few men ever have.

His work was so outstanding that people called him a genius. But he defined genius as "one percent inspiration" (what you can dream in you mind) "and 99 percent perspiration" (what you do through hard work). He believed that hard work paid off and he became known as the man who kept trying.

Thomas Edison died in West Orange, New Jersey, at 84 years of age. He worked tirelessly and did not let his failures hold him back. Because of that determination, he is regarded as the world's greatest inventor and a genuine American hero.

Abraham Lincoln overcame great personal disappointments, saved the Union during the Civil War, and proved to the world that democracy works.

Abraham Lincoln

A solemn crowd of 15,000 people gathered on a wind swept battlefield being dedicated to the 7,500 soldiers who had died there. Governors and congressmen were among the group. The long ceremony neared the end as a famous orator concluded his two-hour-long speech. The president of the United States, Abraham Lincoln, was scheduled to adjourn the gathering. The tall, lanky president stood on the platform and in his high-pitched Kentucky accent spoke for two minutes with words that are considered one of the greatest speeches in American history.

"It is for us to be dedicated to the great task remaining before us . . . that this nation, under God, shall have a new birth of freedom . . . and that government of the people, by the people, for the people, shall not perish from the earth."

These famous words were part of the comments made by Lincoln at Gettysburg, Pennsylvania, on November 19, 1863 during the Civil War.

Abraham Lincoln was one of the great men in American history. He rose from a humble beginning to become the 16th President of the United States.

He accomplished many things including holding the nation together as one during the Civil War and proved to the world that democracy works. Few people realize that his extraordinary achievements were made in spite of many disappointments in his life.

The year was 1809. Thomas and Mary Lincoln lived on a farm near Hodgenville, Kentucky. It was there on February 12, that Abraham Lincoln was born in their log cabin home.

When Abe was a young child, his family lived in several different places. In 1816, they moved to Spencer County in southwest Indiana where Thomas Lincoln bought 160 acres of land from the government. Although Abe was only 8 years old, he was large for his age and had enough strength to swing an ax. He helped his father cut down trees and clear the land so it could be used for farming.

When they could, young Abe and his older sister, Sarah, walked to a log schoolhouse where they learned the basics of reading, writing, and arithmetic. When Abe was 9 years old, his mother died. It was a difficult time for Abe and Sarah as they shared the jobs of keeping house and working the farm. That didn't leave much time to attend school.

A year later, Thomas Lincoln left the children with neighbors and returned to Kentucky for a short visit. There he met an old friend, Sarah Johnson, whose husband had died and left her with three children. They spent time together and talked about their families' situations. Soon they decided to marry. When Thomas Lincoln returned to Indiana, he had a new wife and her three children with him.

Young Abe liked his new mother right away. She saw how much Abe enjoyed learning new things, and she encouraged him to learn all he could.

When his family moved to Macon County, Illinois, in February of 1830, Lincoln was 19. He was six feet and four inches tall with powerful arms and shoulders.

Thomas Lincoln said, "Abe, it will soon be time to leave home and strike out on your own."

"I know," Abe replied.

He looked for the right opportunity, and at age 22 he went to work for a trader named Denton Offutt. They attached logs to build a flatboat and floated the river on a trading voyage to New Orleans.

They stopped along the river to trade items on the boat for items of greater value. For example, they might trade a sack of cornmeal for a farming tool. At the end of their journey, they had supplies which were more valuable than the items they owned when the journey began.

During the trading trip, Lincoln observed the cruel way slaves were treated. In towns along the river he saw beaten Negroes locked in chains and sold like cattle. This haunting sight made a lasting impression on him. He thought about it often.

After the trip to New Orleans, Denton Offutt hired Lincoln to clerk in a store he owned at New Salem, Illinois. When Lincoln arrived there, he described himself as "a piece of floating driftwood." He lived in New Salem for almost six years, from the summer of 1831 until the spring of 1837.

He earned little money and lived in a room at the back of the store. Older women worried about him. "Abe, you don't eat enough to stay alive. I brought you some good home cooking. Eat up, and let me take your clothes and do some mending."

While working at the store, Lincoln earned a reputation for kindness, reliability, and honesty. The job gave him free time that he used to continue his education. He read books on all subjects including the literature of Shakespeare, English grammar, and the principles of law.

Abe became popular for his good humor and storytelling. Customers would come to the store just to sit around and hear him tell stories. He entertained them well.

The study of law held a special interest for Lincoln so he kept up with the politics in the area where he lived. He wanted to know who was running for an office in the legislature and how successful they were after being elected.

Many of his friends who knew he was interested in politics encouraged him to become a candidate for the state legislature.

"Abe, you should run for the state legislature. You know more than the man we last elected. And, we know you can be trusted to do the right thing."

Lincoln thought about the idea a lot. He decided to combine his interest in politics with his popular support. In March 1832, Abe announced that he'd run as a candidate for a seat in the Illinois General Assembly.

He was excited. A broad smile filled his face to match the sparkle in his eyes when he asked people for their votes. But his campaign effort was very limited. He was a member of the Illinois militia, which was called to fight in the Black Hawk War just as his campaign got under way. His military service lasted for only 90 days, but it kept him from campaigning. He arrived back home only two weeks before the election.

He was defeated in that election, but was encouraged when the people in his own area gave him 277 of their 300 votes.

Next, Lincoln used his store clerking experience, and bought a general store in New Salem with William Berry as a partner. Lincoln promised to repay the money he borrowed to start the business.

The store was in trouble when he bought it and didn't get much better afterwards. The business lost money, and after a few months had debts of $1,100. That was a heavy debt at the time, but Lincoln was a man of honor. He kept his word and spent 15 years of hard work to pay off the debt.

Other jobs followed. Lincoln worked as a postmaster where he received and delivered mail. He also worked as a land surveyor making maps of farm land and recorded them so the legal owners of the land could prove it was theirs.

A seat in the state legislature still remained his goal. Deep down inside that was what he wanted to do. He ran for office again in 1834, and he won! Lincoln used his first two-year term to learn how the legislature did its work. He watched, listened, and learned. That effort served him well. In the next six years, he built on that knowledge to become an important leader. Others in the legislature looked to him for ideas and advice.

Things were going well for Lincoln. He was happy and he was in love. Then tragedy came. Ann Rutledge, a young lady he loved, became ill with typhoid fever and died. A dark cloud of sadness covered him. He was so crushed that he lost direction for his life.

John Stuart, a close friend in the state legislature, stayed by his side. He saw how Lincoln was struggling. He encouraged Lincoln to work through his loss and become an attorney. Stuart said, "Abe, you're a fine representative, but you should get your law degree."

Lincoln responded to the challenge. He studied hard, and in September 1836 he received his license to practice law. Then he moved to Springfield to become a junior partner in the law firm of Stuart and Lincoln.

As time passed, Lincoln became a popular lawyer and member of the Illinois State Legislature. He was invited to many of the parties in Springfield. At one party, he met Mary Todd who had moved from Lexington, Kentucky, to live with her married sister in Springfield. Mary was well educated and had a special interest in politics. When she met Lincoln, he described himself as "a poor nobody." She didn't think so, and the common interest in politics brought them together.

The relationship between Abe Lincoln and Mary Todd was off and on for several months, but she continued to encourage him to pursue politics. She even predicted, "He will be President of the United States one day. You can see that he is not pretty. But doesn't he look as if he would make a magnificent president?"

They continued dating and finally married in 1842. Lincoln was 33, and Mary was 23. They later had four sons born to them in Springfield, but only Robert Todd, the oldest son, lived past childhood. The other three sons died as young children. That brought great grief to both Mary and Abe—more sadness and another disappointment to overcome.

In 1847, Lincoln left behind his state legislature job and campaigned for a position in the United States Congress. He won! Nearly everyone in his district voted for him. He was delighted!

Lincoln was eager to be a good congressman. The issue of slavery got his attention. The haunting memory of mistreated slaves was still with him. He worked hard to get laws passed that would end slavery in the District of Columbia; the very place where congress met. He knew that was the right thing to do but many congressmen did not agree.

His personal campaign against slavery made him so unpopular that he did not seek re-election when his term ended in 1849. Disappointed with congress, Lincoln looked for other places to work. He applied for the job as head of the General Land Office, which he didn't get.

Disappointed again, Lincoln returned to Springfield to practice law more earnestly than ever. He took more difficult cases that were tried before the high courts. He won those cases and became well known for his success.

Lincoln was making a name for himself when the topic of slavery came up again. That grabbed his attention, and he soon was back into politics. The Missouri Compromise, a law passed in 1820, made it unlawful to own slaves in the new western territories of the United States.

But early in 1854, Senator Stephen Douglas of Illinois introduced a bill to allow settlers in the new territories of Kansas and Nebraska to decide for themselves whether or not they wanted slavery. If settlers voted "yes," then slavery would spread.

Lincoln believed slavery was an injustice and a bad practice. He wanted to keep it from spreading. This was his opportunity to get involved.

Mary Todd Lincoln said, "Abe, why don't you campaign for the senate seat held by Stephen Douglas? Defeat him, and stop his push to extend slavery into the new territories."

Lincoln made no reply

"You can do it, Abe."

"Mary, it's hard to defeat a senator who is already in office."

"You've got to try," Mary insisted.

"You're right, Mary. I've got to try."

Lincoln entered the 1854 campaign for the U.S. Senate and opposed Senator Douglas throughout Illinois for his party's nomination. Because Douglas was already in office, Lincoln failed to get his party's nomination, dropped out of the race, and gave his support to another candidate. He thought, *if I can't get nominated, I will at least help someone else get elected.*

In 1856 Lincoln took a different approach. He joined the new Republican Party, the political party that opposed slavery. He worked hard for the Republican candidates who were trying to be elected. Because of his hard work for others, he became well known and appreciated by leaders in the Republican Party. As a result, the Republican Party chose Lincoln to campaign against Douglas in the U.S. Senate race of 1858. Here was another attempt to defeat Douglas.

Lincoln attacked Douglas's position on slavery. During the campaign Lincoln said, "A house divided against itself cannot stand. I believe this government cannot endure permanently half slave and half free."

Lincoln challenged Douglas to a series of seven debates. They moved from one town to the next, wherever people would gather to hear them. Lincoln spoke against slavery because he regarded it "as a moral, social, and political evil."

"Slavery is a moral, social, and political evil."

Men were elected to congress differently then than they are now. Then, the Illinois state legislature elected the man for the U.S. Senate seat. The state was divided into districts in such a way that Douglas supporters were able to elect and send Douglas back to Congress. Lincoln lost. Another defeat. Another disappointment.

Although he did not win the Senate seat, the debates with Douglas brought Lincoln to the attention of the nation. He used the time from 1858-1860 to continue making speeches that explained his political views. More people listened to his opinion about slavery. Many agreed with what he said.

The Republican National Convention met in Chicago in May of 1860, to choose the man they would support for president. Lincoln, nicknamed the "Rail-splitter" by his supporters, was very popular. People were turning to him as their leader, and he won the party's nomination.

Lincoln went on the road and battled his old rival, Senator Douglas, this time in the presidential campaign. Lincoln used every speech to give his views on what the nation needed. Voters liked what he stood for and gave him their votes. Lincoln won the national election that fall with most of his support coming from the North. His election was an exciting victory, but it created turmoil for the nation.

During the few months between Lincoln's election and when he took office, seven southern states withdrew from the Union. The nation suddenly faced a serious crisis.

In February of 1861, Lincoln said farewell to his friends in Springfield. "I now leave with a task before me greater than that which rested upon Washington. Without the assistance of the Divine Being who attended him, I cannot succeed. With that assistance, I cannot fail."

In the South four million people were held in slavery. Slave owners lived in constant fear that those in bondage would attempt an uprising and try to break free. To deal with the threat, they organized militias that were armed, drilled, and trained to keep the threat in check. If a conflict with the North started, they would have thousands of well-trained soldiers enlisted and ready to fight.

Lincoln took the oath of office in March 1861 and became the 16th President of the United States. He spoke that day urging the states to stay together. But he warned that he would use the full power of his office to "hold, occupy, and possess the properties and places belonging to the federal government."

The South ignored the warning. They quickly took control of federal forts within the southern states. Lincoln had to make a tough decision. Should he retake the forts? He stood looking out the French doors in his office. In the gathering darkness of the night, he imagined an approaching storm of conflict.

Fort Sumter at Charleston, South Carolina, became the test. If Lincoln withdrew the Union troops, the North would protest. If he reinforced the fort, the South would consider it an act of war.

As a compromise, Lincoln decided to send only food to the fort when supplies ran low. Confederate leaders in South Carolina did not consider it a compromise. They replied in anger and demanded the surrender of the fort. The Union fort commander refused. Confederate artillery opened fire. The Civil War had started; it was April, 1861.

To Lincoln, the United States was an example of how people could govern themselves. The entire world watched. Could he prove to the world that democracy works? This was the test. Would the nation remain as one? Or, would it split into two parts?

Lincoln said, "If we do not make common cause to save the good old ship of the Union on this voyage, nobody will have a chance to pilot her on another voyage."

More American lives were lost during the Civil War
than any other war in American history.

The Union army was called out. They were well prepared for battle. They expected a swift victory but at the first Battle of Bull Run, the Confederate troops had a big win. People then realized that the war would be a long one.

The Civil War actually became four long years of bloodshed and took more American lives than any other war in American history. Three million Americans fought in it and more than 600,000 men died in it! Hundreds of thousands more were wounded or hurt.

As the war dragged on, Lincoln took action to abolish slavery. He issued the Emancipation Proclamation. It stated that slaves in the Confederate territory would be free on January 1, 1863. Lincoln urged people in the Border States between the North and South to free their slaves, and he asked the states to pay the owners for their losses. He promised financial help from the federal government. Slave holding states did not cooperate.

Fighting continued with both sides winning battles. Places became well known such as Williamsburg, Bull Run, Petersburg, Shiloh, Harper's Ferry, and many others. Victories by the Union army at Gettysburg and Vicksburg became the turning point of the war.

The war was winding down as the presidential election was held in the fall of 1864. Lincoln was re-elected. He felt the end of the war was near, and he wanted to reunite the nation. In his second inaugural address he asked for "malice toward none and charity for all." He encouraged the people "to bind up the nation's wounds and do all to achieve a just and lasting peace."

The difficult war years brought a constant challenge to Lincoln. Horace Greeley wrote at the time, "He slowly won his way to fame by doing the work that lay next to him . . . doing it with all his growing might . . . doing it as well as he could and learning by his failure how to do it better."

The Confederate surrender took place in Virginia

The war ended on April 9, 1865, when Confederate General Robert E. Lee surrendered to General Ulysses S. Grant at Appomattox Court House in Virginia. While Generals Grant and Lee were inside the courthouse signing documents, two soldiers milled around the courtyard.

The Federal soldier said, "You Johnny Rebs kept this thing going a long time."

"Us southern boys don't run from a fight."

The two looked at each other for several moments. "I lost my best friend at Bull Run," spoke the Federal.

"My brother was killed at Vicksburg, and my cousin lost a leg," countered the Confederate.

The Federal moved a little closer and asked, "What are you going to do now?"

"Headin' home, I guess, if there's anything left to go home to."

"Well, it's over now."

"Yeah, Yank, it's over. But we ain't fergetten."

The nation did not divide into two parts. It remained as one. Five days later on April 14, Lincoln held a long cabinet meeting to discuss plans of how to bring the nation back together.

That evening Lincoln, his wife, and friends attended a play at Ford's Theater in Washington.

John Wilkes Booth, a young actor with piercing eyes and dark curly hair, hid in the shadows of the theater. Booth was a fanatical supporter of the Southern cause. As the audience focused their attention on the play, Booth slipped upstairs and stopped outside the president's box. He pulled back the curtains, silently moved up behind Lincoln, and fired a bullet into his head. Booth yelled, "The South is avenged." He jumped from the balcony to the stage below and escaped.

People ran for the exits yelling and screaming. Help arrived for the president who was quickly moved to a house across the street. He remained unconscious as doctors did all they could to save his life. Friends stood by throughout the night, worrying and waiting. The gun shot was fatal. Lincoln died at 7:22 a.m. the next morning.

A touching ceremony, filled with emotion, was held at the White House in Washington. The body, carried along Pennsylvania Avenue to the Capitol, was escorted to the Baltimore train station and started on the solemn 1,654 mile journey across America.

Edwin Stanton, a member of the Lincoln cabinet, expressed the feeling of many; "Now he belongs to the ages."

Millions of people grieved his death. They stood in weeping silence along the rail tracks to pay their respects as the train carried his body from Washington to Springfield, Illinois, where it was buried in Oak Ridge Cemetery.

Through the years Lincoln has continued to be an inspiration to people of all ages. One of the qualities that made Lincoln such a great man and president was the way he responded to the personal disappointments in his life.

Individuals today study his life but fail to realize the many difficulties he overcame.

Look back over Lincoln's life and recall these challenging times.
- His mother died when he was 9.
- He was defeated for the Illinois legislature in 1832.
- His general store business failed.
- Ann Rutledge died in 1835.
- He lost support for re-election to Congress in 1849 because of his stand on slavery.
- Three of his four sons died while they were still young children.
- He failed to get the job as Commissioner of the General Land Office in 1849.

Lincoln is an inspiration to people everywhere.

- He was unable to get his party's nomination in the United States Senate race in 1854.
- He was defeated in the United States Senate race in 1858.
- Seven Southern states withdrew from the Union after his election as President in 1860.
- He was the nation's leader during The Civil War that brought death and misery to the North and South.

As the 16th President of the United States, Lincoln led the nation through the dark days of the Civil War and preserved the Union. Lincoln overcame many obstacles and never gave up. He remains an inspiration to people everywhere.

Sequoyah invented an alphabet so his Cherokee Nation could learn to read and write.

Sequoyah

The early morning mist lifted as the sun appeared through the trees and people began to move around the Indian village. It seemed like a normal day, but it wasn't. Something very important was about to take place.

The Cherokee Nation's Tribal Council had been sent word that they needed to meet. Council members had come from distant villages, spent the night, and now were gathering in the meeting lodge.

In the center of the council sat an Indian man and his 6-year-old daughter. If they were afraid, their faces did not show it. They sat up straight and remained calm.

This council meeting was very important. It would affect the life of each person in the Cherokee nation.

But let's back up. The story actually began around 1770, in the Cherokee nation's territory known today as Tennessee.

The Cherokees lived in cabins, farmed the land, raised cattle, and even welcomed the white traders who came into their territory. That is how a trader named Gist met and married an Indian girl who became the mother of Sequoyah.

One day Gist left his family to go on a trading mission; however, he never returned. Was he alive? Did he move to another part of the country? No one ever knew.

It was tough for Sequoyah to grow up without a father, but his mother loved him very much. She took very good care of him. Sequoyah walked with a limp as a result of an accident or illness early in his childhood. That might explain why he spent a lot of time by himself in the woods where he made sketches of all the animals he saw around him. As he grew older, he became an excellent silversmith who was well known for the jewelry he made.

Other Cherokee Indians teased and made fun of Sequoyah.

One day in 1812, officers from the American army came to his Indian village. They asked for volunteers to fight the Creek Indians who had joined with the British to fight the Americans. Sequoyah, along with other Cherokee Indians, joined the American army.

While in the army, Sequoyah noticed the expression on the faces of soldiers as they read letters from home. That seemed strange to him. He thought, *what are they doing that makes them look so happy?* He didn't understand what the letters were. The more he watched, the more he believed that these "talking leaves" had an importance that set the white men apart. His Indian friends believed there was magic in the way a white man could tell others what he was thinking by making marks on a piece of paper.

Sequoyah told his friends that the Cherokees could also have their own "talking leaves." They laughed, teased, and made fun of him. He thought, *I know the Indians can have talking leaves, too. I'm going to figure it out.*

After his army service, Sequoyah returned home where he spent most of his time working on the method of talking leaves. He neglected the farm which was soon covered with weeds. His neighbors said, "You are wasting your time." Others said he was either lazy or a little crazy. Although people said bad things about him, Sequoyah continued his work.

His work caused difficulty even with his family. He built a cabin apart from them so he could better concentrate. One day a slammed door broke his focus. Startled, Sequoyah looked up to see his wife enter the cabin. She threw all his sketches and writing tools into the fire in the fireplace.

"You crazy Indian. Stop wasting time on this big idea of yours," she shouted.

Sequoia's work was destroyed, but he started over. He thought, *no one believes in me but this work must continue.*

A mood of sadness fell over the cabin, but he continued his work with no other person to encourage or help him. With no one to talk to him and unable to read, he simply worked alone. He did have a clear goal that guided him. He was determined to give his people a way to read and write.

Sequoyah at first thought he could make a mark or character for each word in the Cherokee language. But there were too many words. He soon realized that idea would not work.

One day Sequoyah saw something lying beside the road. Walking over for a close look, he picked it up to examine it more closely. It was an English spelling book containing words he had never seen before. He had another idea. Although he did not know a single English letter, he used many of the letters to represent sounds in the Cherokee language. He then divided the Cherokee words into sounds and assigned a character to each sound.

Sequoyah struggled to divide his time between working the farm and his special project. Twelve years of trial and error finally produced 86 different characters that could be used to represent all the sounds in the Cherokee language. The characters were different from each other, easy to read, and could be written quickly.

Even after Sequoyah completed the 86 character alphabet, he had great difficulty proving to others that the discovery was worthwhile. He was excited, but no one else seemed to care. His six-year-old daughter was the only one who showed real interest in his work.

During a visit with friends in Arkansas, Sequoyah taught them to use his discovery. He said, "Use these letters, and write to your friends in Mississippi. I'll carry the message back for them to read."

Sequoyah carried the sealed letter back to Mississippi and read it to the man's friends. They were shocked. Here, sealed in paper, were words in the Cherokee language all the way from Arkansas.

"Sequoyah, this is big magic."

Sequoyah smiled.

"You must share this magic with the council."

"I know. A few of our people realize we now have 'talking leaves', but the council must accept it." Sequoyah made plans to address them.

Years later Sequoyah looked back to remember that council meeting that changed everything.

The Cherokee Council was made up of old and wise men. They made decisions that affected the entire Cherokee nation. The council sat dressed in colorful clothes decorated with beads. Some wore headbands filled with long feathers. This was a solemn faced group; serious, no-nonsense.

The council waited silently until Sequoyah and his six-year-old daughter came into room. Father and daughter sat up straight and looked at the council members. If they were afraid, they didn't show it.

The council leader said, "Take the daughter from the room to a far distance where no sounds of our talk can be heard."

A young Cherokee led the girl from the room. They walked down a trail where honeysuckle grew thick, and its sweet smell helped to calm the little girl's pounding heart.

The chief spoke words and phrases which Sequoyah wrote down. Then they called in his daughter to read what was written.

The little girl felt fear and excitement, but she remained calm and read aloud the exact words written by her father.

71

Sequoyah and his daughter faced the tribal council
of the Cherokee nation.

Council members glanced at each other without comment, only a slight nod of the head.

Then Sequoyah was taken outside, his daughter wrote as instructed. Again the result was the same. The Indian Council was amazed and completely satisfied. They realized they were in the presence of someone extraordinary. A smile spread across their faces. They said, "We must test this on others."

The council selected a group of young men for Sequoyah to teach. The group was happy to be selected and learned quickly. The council tested them in the same way they had tested Sequoyah. The results were the same. Now the Cherokee nation could use a written language to pass on the story of their people. Their rich history and traditions would now be written for the first time. Now their stories would not be lost. The legends of the Cherokee Rose, legend of the Wren, the story of the First Woman, plus many other traditional stories would be written and passed to each new generation.

In a short time the Cherokees became a reading nation. Each person who learned to read took the time to teach someone else. All of Sequoyah's hard work had paid off. To express its gratitude, The Cherokee nation presented Sequoyah with a medal which he wore proudly around his neck.

Sequoyah's alphabet was used to teach the Cherokee Nation to read and write.

Sequoyah was honored in many ways for his work. One special honor occurred in 1849. The great redwood trees in California were named as a living memorial to him. It is indeed fitting that these Sequoia trees, some 3,500 years old, are an ageless honor to the lasting contribution of this American Indian.

Through determination and hard work, Sequoyah invented an alphabet which was used to teach his people to read and write. In doing so, he accomplished his goal in life.

Harriet Tubman escaped slavery and risked her life to escort Southern slaves to freedom in the North.

Harriet Tubman

The winter night was so cold, chilling from head to toe. The men who patrolled the back roads looking for slaves would not be out tonight. There was no moonlight either. The sky was dark; black as a piece of coal. What a perfect night to escape!

Slaves huddled in their tiny cabins could not sleep. They didn't talk, just waited. The only sound was a whine that came from wind blowing through the trees outside. But they waited for a different sound. A signal, low and soft, just above a whisper. Their thoughts were the same, *will this be the night she comes for us?*

They listened for her signal. When it came, each of them slipped out of the cabin and move to the grove of trees down the road. The person waiting for them was Harriet Tubman. The slaves called her "Moses" because she would lead them from slavery to freedom in the North.

This remarkable story of Harriet Tubman started around 1820. Her exact birth date is unknown, but her parents were slaves living in Maryland's Dorchester County.

Harriet was only 6 years old when she was taken from her mother and sent to work for a white family who lived on a farm ten miles away. She was assigned many tasks around the farm. At 8 years of age, she took care of a baby all day and night. Every time the baby cried Harriet was beaten.

As she got older, Harriet learned to do all types of work. She learned household chores such as baking and sewing. She also learned the rough physical jobs of driving oxen, plowing, and cutting timber.

Slaves did not learn how to do things from reading books because it was unlawful to teach a slave to read. But slaves knew very well how to do the everyday chores around a farm.

They also had meaningful traditions and superstitions which they passed from one generation to another. Many of the white owners placed their children in the care of older slave women who had a strong influence on the children especially through the stories the slaves told. The slave could not punish the white children so they used stories to either entertain the children or scare them into good behavior.

One day on Harriet's plantation the older slave that cared for the children was ill. Some believe that Harriet was assigned the older slave's task for a few days. Harriet asked the older woman for advice.

"I ain't done this before. Those chil'en goin'a act out and get me in trouble. What'a I do?"

The older slave said, "Let me tell you what'a do cause this will work just fine." She chuckled as she told Harriet the story of special ghost called the "Boogy Man." He was the ghost who would get you if you were naughty.

Later in the day Harriet took the children to the edge of the woods and sat them on the ground around a small campfire. Everything was quiet. No noise was heard except the crackle of the fire.

Harriet spoke in a soft, slow voice just above a whisper. The children sat still as a stone and leaned forward to hear each word. Then suddenly a frightful figure jumped out from the darkness dressed all in white with red paint on his black face. He shook a gourd with pebbles inside; the turkey feathers stuck in his hair bounced side to side.

The creature pranced around the group then stopped dead still. Nothing moved during a long silence. Then with a scream the creature jumped at the children with stretched out arms; chicken feet claws tied to his fingers.

Harriet yelled, "Boogy man, dat's de Boogy Man!"

The ghost was actually a dressed up slave. With their hearts beating wildly and their voices screaming loudly, the children ran to the big house as fast as their little legs could go. The little children laid awake that night listening to all the night noises. And just as they drifted off to sleep, they thought they heard a voice whisper, "De Boogy Man gonna get ya if you don't watch out!"

Like many others, Harriet endured hard times throughout her slavery days. One incident left her injured for life.

A slave from her plantation ran away but was caught and brought back. The owner said, "I'll teach you to run away. Harriet, hold him down. I'm going to whip him 'til he can't stand up."

Harriett thought, *I can't do this. I can't help to get him whipped.* She didn't move.

The slave seeing his chance made a dash for the door. The owner grabbed a two-pound iron weight and threw it at the man. Harriet who was standing by the door was accidentally hit on the head. The blow knocked her unconscious and affected her throughout her life. It often caused her to fall sound asleep even while she sat talking to a friend.

Harriet's owner died in 1849, and she knew she would be sold to someone else. She thought, w*hat is going to happen to me now? What will the new owner be like? Will I be moved to another state?*

She asked a friend, "What you think we gotta do?"
"Nothing we can do."

After a long silence, Harriet said, "I'm gonna run."

"Harriet, you'll never make it. Patrol gonna catch ya. They'll whip you good."

"Gotta take da chance. Can't stay here no mo," Harriet said with a determined look on her face.

Escaping from a plantation was almost impossible but Harriet was ready for the risk.

Harriet hid in a wagon and covered herself with sacks of grain.

She made her plan and waited for the right time. She waited and waited. Then when the time was just right, she left on a Saturday night hoping not to be missed until Monday morning. It was a dark night; very little light from the moon. She moved through the woods out of sight of the men who patrolled the roads, followed the North Star, and headed for Pennsylvania.

She said later, "I had reasoned this out in my mind; there was one of two things I had a right to; liberty or death. If I could not have one, I would have the other."

Harriet knew the great risk in trying to escape slavery, but she believed people along the way would help her. She was right!

A white neighbor told her about an escape route; about places and people who would hide her.

"Harriet, stay here until its dark. There'll be enough moonlight for you to see your way through the woods. You'll come to a creek. Follow it upstream about five miles, and you'll see a farmhouse with a rusted lantern hanging on the fence out front. That's your next stop."

"How I know it's safe?" Harriet asked.

"The rusted lantern is a sign of a safe house."

Harriet asked, "Are there other signs I need to know?"

"Yes, during the day you'll see a quilt hanging over the front porch railings. It'll contain sections of cloth in different shapes. Each shape has a different message."

"What kind of message?"

"The signs will tell you if it's safe to travel on. But the folks at the next safe house will explain all that to you."

Harriett found the next safe house and was hidden. The next day she was placed in a wagon, covered with sacks of grain, and moved to the next secret location. The escape route was called the Underground Railroad. It helped Southern slaves flee to the North.

Harriet made her way to Philadelphia where she used her skills to find work and save some money. She said, "I had crossed the line of which I had so long been dreaming. I was free!"

The next year Harriet became part of the Underground Railroad. She wanted to use what she knew to help other slaves escape. She became a "conductor," the person who led Southern slaves to freedom. Escaping slaves were called "passengers." The hiding places along the way were called "stations." Wagons were used a lot to transport the slaves. Many had false bottoms where runaways could hide. Sometimes they were hidden under sacks of grain or loads of vegetables.

Most escapes that Harriet led took place in the winter months when the nights were long and the roads were empty. She always followed the same plan she had used herself. The journey started on Saturday night because most slaves were allowed to visit friends from Saturday night until Monday morning. Their absence would not be noticed until around noon on Monday. Then it would be Tuesday before a runaway notice could be posted.

A successful escape required all the tricks that Harriet had learned. Wanted posters describing the slaves would be nailed to trees along the dirt roads that people traveled. Harriet sometimes hired a man to follow the person who posted the notices and tear the posters down when no one was watching.

Many times when slave owners were catching up to them, she turned her group around and headed south. She told her group, "Huddle up, and stay close to me. We're turning around and heading back the way we came. It will confuse them. They will go on by us, and then we can hide and start again."

This was a perfect night to escape.

Small children always added to the danger. They would sometimes cry when the group was hiding, which put everyone at risk. Harriet handled that problem, too. She pulled a bottle from her bag and gave children a mild drug to make them sleep. The group would hide in the woods, covered with leaves, and remain motionless until Harriet gave the signal to move on.

In one place, Harriet hid her group in the woods while she went into town to buy food. Entering the area near the general store, she stopped in her tracks when she heard two men talking. They stood beside a tree on which an escape poster was nailed. The poster described her and offered of a large reward for her capture.

"Jim, what are you hanging around here for?"

"I figured on making me some money....big money."

"You won't get any just standing around."

"Look at this wanted poster. Some of the planters must want that slave pretty badly to pay that kind of money to get her back."

Jim said, "With $40,000 I could have my own plantation, slaves and all."

Harriet stood nearby and listened.

"Says here this runaway can't read or write. That ought to make it easier for me to figure out who she is. Her group has gotta eat. Not many places to get grub so I'll just hang out here and wait."

Harriet had heard enough. She had to get food for her group and move them on. But she also had to avoid being captured. She hesitated for only a moment then pulled a book from her bag. Pretending to read, she walked past the men and into the supply store. Her heart was pounding, but she walked along at a normal pace. They looked carefully at her as she passed by but did nothing. *Wow! Another close call!* Harriet thought.

A $40,000 reward for her capture.

By now Harriet was famous as the leader of slaves escaping to the North. If caught, she would be punished, tortured, and possibly killed. But her courage and unique ability to sense danger kept her free.

During a ten-year period from 1850–1860, she made nineteen trips into the South and escorted more than 300 slaves to freedom. And, as she said on one occasion, "I never lost a single one!"

When the Civil War started in 1861, Harriet Tubman participated as a spy and scout for the Union Army. She gathered valuable information from slaves in the South and passed it along to army officers. She also shared her knowledge of the back roads and woods. She even served as a nurse and showed equal concern for both Northern and Southern soldiers who were wounded.

Harriet lived in Auburn, New York, after the war. There she met and worked with Susan B. Anthony in the fight for women's right to vote. She also used her many skills to earn a living and gave most of her money to the poor.

Harriet Tubman lived into her nineties and died at her home on March 10, 1913. Friends gathered around her bed sang the spiritual, "Swing Low, Sweet Chariot."

Today, thousands of Americans admire this brave woman who risked her life to escort slaves to freedom. They remember her determination. They marvel at her skill of escape. They feel her presence even now when they read her words spoken many years ago;

"I looked at my hands to see if I was the same person now that I am free. There was such a glory over everything; the sun came like gold through the trees, and over the fields, and I felt like I was in Heaven."

Resource Information

The Battle of Bull Run took place in northeast Virginia southwest from Washington, D.C. It was the place of two important Civil War battles both won by the Confederate Army.

Carpet-bagger was a Northerner who went to the South following the Civil War and sought political or financial gain through unfair means. They were given the name because the person carried his belongings in a carpetbag.

The Civil War, also referred to as the War Between the States, began on April 12, 1861 and ended on May 26, 1865. It was a military conflict between the United States of America [the Union] and the Confederate States of America [the Confederacy]. The chief cause of the war was slavery. Southern states depended on slavery to support their economy. The main debate in the days before the war was whether slavery would be permitted to spread into the new Western territories.

Committees of the House of Representatives total 19 and most of these have subcommittees. The committees are very powerful because the House of Representatives usually accepts their recommendations. The House Ways and Means Committee is one of the five most powerful.

Constitutional Amendments are made by one of two methods. Congress may, by a two-thirds vote in each house, propose a constitutional amendment. It must then be ratified by three-quarters of the state legislatures. In the other method of amendments, two-thirds of the states may call a constitutional convention. Amendments proposed at this convention must then be ratified by three-fourths of the states. This second method has never been used.

Amendment 13 abolished slavery in all states. Lincoln's Emancipation Proclamation applied only to slavery in states that had seceded from the Union.

Amendment 14 states that anyone born or naturalized in the United States is a citizen. The amendment shifted power from the states to the federal government, giving the federal government authority to enforce individual rights against the states.

Amendment 19 gave women the right to vote. The Constitution never prohibited women from voting and for many years before this amendment, women did vote in some states. The 19th Amendment established a uniform rule for all states to follow in guaranteeing women this right.

The Dred Scott Case added to tensions before the Civil War. Dred Scott, a slave, sued for his freedom on the ground that his owner had taken him to free territory where he should not be considered a slave. The Supreme Court ruled that Scott did not have the right to file suit because he was not a citizen of the United States. As a slave he was considered property. The justices wrote that congress had no power to keep slavery from the territories; therefore the Missouri Compromise and other legislation limiting slavery were unconstitutional.

The Emancipation Proclamation issued by Abraham Lincoln on January 1, 1863, during the Civil War, declared that slaves within any state in rebellion would be free. It took enactment of the 13th Amendment to the Constitution before slavery ended in all states.

The Ku Klux Klan is a secret organization that originated in the southern states following the Civil War. It directed activities against leaders, governments, and individuals who supported the rise of former slaves to a status of equal citizenship. Wearing robes, masks and pointed hoods, they terrorized victims by burning crosses on front lawns, burning homes, and beating and murdering their victims.

The Missouri Compromise resulted when Missouri, a slave state, sought admission to the Union. Opponents of slavery tried to keep slavery from spreading. To keep the balance in the Senate, the decision was made to admit Missouri as a slave state and admit Maine as a free state. A line was drawn from Missouri's northern boundary, and slavery would not be allowed in territory north of that line.

Patent is a grant made by the government that gives the creator of an invention the sole right to make, use, and sell that invention for a set period of time without interference from others.

Sequoia National Forest, named in honor of Sequoyah, the Cherokee Indian, is a forest of giant redwood trees found on the western slopes of the Sierra Nevada in central California. One tree known as the General Sherman is 273 feet tall, 101 feet in circumference and about 3,500 years old.

The Slave Trade involved the kidnapping of individuals mostly from the region of western Africa. They were then transported by ship to America where they were sold as workers for manual and domestic labor.

Elizabeth C. Stanton was social reformer and activist for women's rights. She helped organize the first women's rights convention in 1848. She worked closely with Susan Anthony, writing most of the material used in the women's movement.

The Temperance Movement in the United States was directed against the manufacture, sale, and drinking of intoxicating liquors.

The Underground Railroad was the codeword for the escape route used by Southern slaves to reach freedom in the North.

Praise for *They Never Gave Up*

"I see a great need for today's children to understand the value of overcoming difficulties and becoming contributing citizens. This book is an excellent resource for classroom teachers all across our country." Dr. Betsy Rodgers—2003 National Teacher of the Year.

"Superb presentation will encourage and inspire children" Dr. Carden Johnston—former president of the American Academy of Pediatrics.

"The stories are as well written as they are inspiring. These real-life vignettes are as exciting as the best fiction on the market for this age group." Tom Bailey—editor of the Alabama Roots Biography Series.

"This book is action driven and emphasizes important lessons of self worth, overcoming difficulties, personal character and values." Wayne Flynt—author of Pulitzer Prize nominated *Poor but Proud: Alabama's Poor Whites*

"Excellent leads that hook the reader at the beginning of each biography and great concluding paragraphs. Exciting color illustrations. Excellent Related Resource Section and Table of Contents." Elise Blackerby—5th grade teacher at a National Blue Ribbon School.

"Great book for 4–6th graders and also lends itself to a teacher read-aloud in lower grades. Good addition to our character education curriculum. Excellent vocabulary for middle readers: text has a fluid flow. Good length in chapters and book. Outstanding illustrations are appropriate for the text and audience." Cleo Lackey—librarian at a National Blue Ribbon School.

Excellent curriculum resource for 4-7th grade students who are studying this same period of American history.
Books are available at Amazon.com. Large quantities are available from the author/publisher. For more information contact:

The Resource Group
3736 Brookwood Road
Birmingham, AL 35223